Opening My Imagination

J'ouvre Mon Imagination

Jayana Wood

Published by Cheryl Wood Empowers
8787 Branch Avenue | Suite 213 | Clinton, MD 20735
301-395-7589 | www.cherylwoodempowers.com

Book design copyright © 2013 by Cheryl Wood Empowers. All rights reserved.
Cover design by Jayana Wood

Published in the United States of America
ISBN 978-1-4675-8123-3
Juvenile non-fiction

This book is ideal for emergent, new and eager youth readers.

Ce livre est idéal pour les émergents, les nouvelles et désireux jeunes lecteurs.

Lalah,

Think Positive

Build Self Love

Create Big Dreams!

I.W.

Travaille dur et pense grand!

(Work hard and dream big!)

Dedication
To my mom, my dad, and my two little brothers, James and Jalen.

Dédicace
A ma maman, mon papa, et mes deux petits freres, James and Jalen.

Sometimes I lie in bed imagining what I can do or become. My mom and dad tell me that the sky is the limit. My mom and dad also tell me to do what I love to do and to do something that makes me smile.

Parfois quand je suis couchée dans mon lit j'imagine qu'est ce que je voudrai devenir. Ma mere et mon pere me dissent le ciel est le limite. Ma mere et mon pere me dissent de faire ce que j'aimerai faire, et de faire quelque chose qui me fait sourire.

Sometimes I imagine myself as a **ballerina**.

Parfois je m'imagine en temps que **danseuse**.

Sometimes I imagine myself as a **baker**.

Parfois je m'imagine en temps que **boulangere**.

Sometimes I imagine myself as an **artist**.

Parfois je m'imagine en temps que **artiste**.

Sometimes I imagine myself as a **firefighter**.

Parfois je m'imagine en temps que **pompier**.

Sometimes I imagine myself as a **teacher**.

Parfois je m'imagine en temps que **professeur**.

Sometimes I imagine myself as
a **fashion designer**.

Parfois je m'imagine en temps
que **styliste**.

Sometimes I imagine myself as a **marine biologist**.

Parfois je m'imagine en temps que **biologiste marine**.

Sometimes I imagine myself as a **pilot**.

Parfois je m'imagine en temps que **pilote**.

Sometimes I imagine myself as
a **doctor**.

Parfois je m'imagine en temps
que **docteur**.

Sometimes I imagine myself as a **florist**.

Parfois je m'imagine en temps que **fleuriste**.

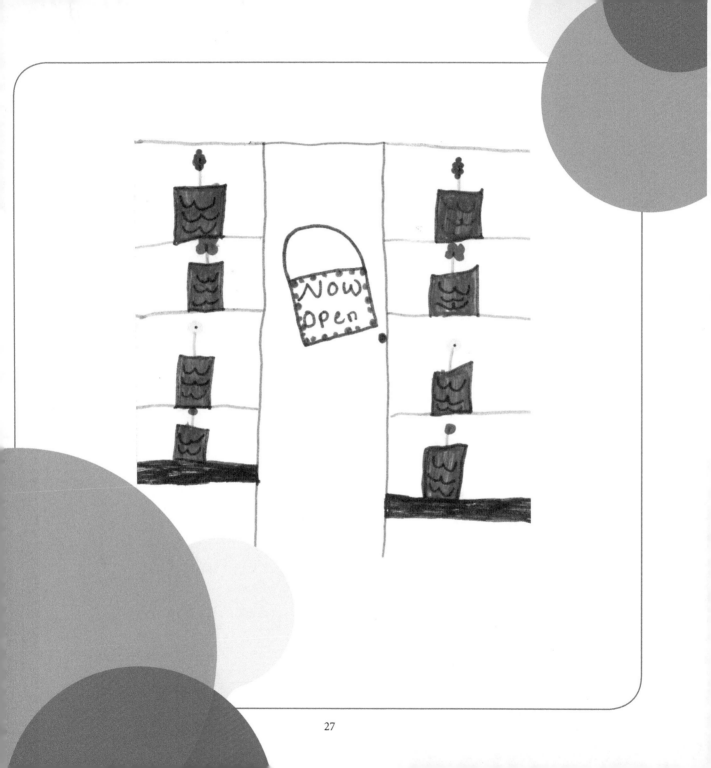

Sometimes I imagine myself as a **singer**.

Parfois je m'imagine en temps que **chanteuse**.

Sometimes I imagine myself as a **police officer**.

Parfois je m'imagine en temps que **agent de police**.

Sometimes I imagine myself as a **poet**.

Parfois je m'imagine en temps que un **poéte**.

Roses are red
and Violets are blue,
first I give you a hug
and then I say "I love
You".

Les roses sont rouges et
les violettes sont bleues,
d'abord je donne un câlin et
puis je dis "Je vous aime."

Sometimes I imagine myself as a **journalist**.

Parfois je m'imagine en temps que **journaliste**.

Sometimes I imagine myself as a **scientist**.

Parfois je m'imagine en temps que **scientifique**.

What do you imagine becoming?

Que-ce-que tu imagines devenir?

The sky is the limit!

Le ciel est le limite!

Message from the Author

To all the kids out there, I just want to say that you do not have to wait until you are 20 or older to do what you really want to do. I'm only nine and I'm writing my first book.

Please don't waste your life eating candy, playing video games, and watching TV. There's so much more to life. Trust me: I know.

The End

Pour tous ces enfants là-bas, je veux juste vous dire que vous n'avez pas à attendre jusqu'a ce que vous avez 20 ans ou plus pour faire ce que vous voulez vraiment faire. J'ai juste neuf ans et j'ecris mon premier livre.

S'il vous plaît ne perdez pas votre temps à manger des bonbons, ou a jouer aux jeux video, ou à regardez la télévision. La vie est plus que ça. Croyez-moi: je le sais.

Fin

In honor of my Grandad David Swann

WE LOVE YOU!
WE MISS YOU!